Shadows and Reflections

Robin Johnson and Douglas Hicton

LIGHTBOX
openlightbox.com

LIGHTBOX

Go to
www.openlightbox.com
and enter this book's unique code.

ACCESS CODE

LBXM2883

Lightbox is an all-inclusive digital solution for the teaching and learning of curriculum topics in an original, groundbreaking way. Lightbox is based on National Curriculum Standards.

OPTIMIZED FOR

- ✓ TABLETS
- ✓ WHITEBOARDS
- ✓ COMPUTERS
- ✓ AND MUCH MORE!

STANDARD FEATURES OF LIGHTBOX

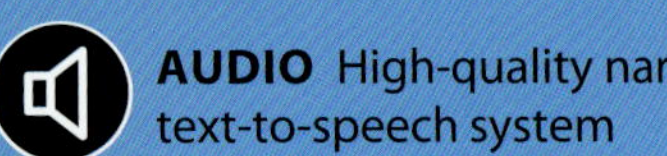
AUDIO High-quality narration using text-to-speech system

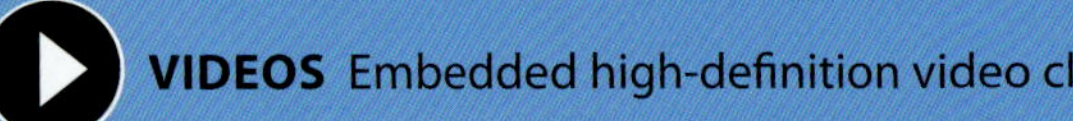
VIDEOS Embedded high-definition video clips

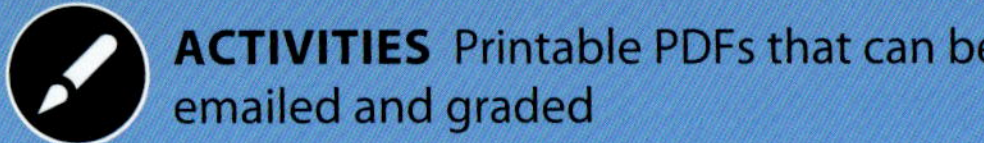
ACTIVITIES Printable PDFs that can be emailed and graded

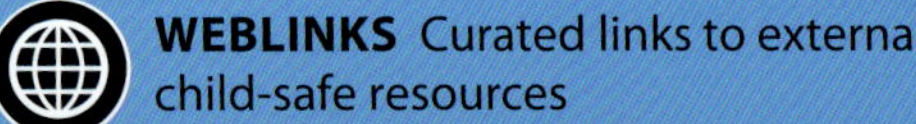
WEBLINKS Curated links to external, child-safe resources

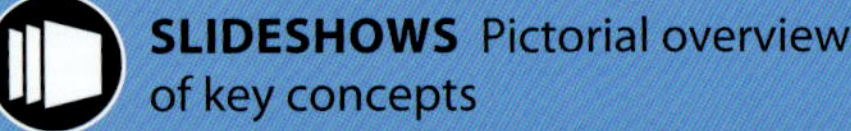
SLIDESHOWS Pictorial overviews of key concepts

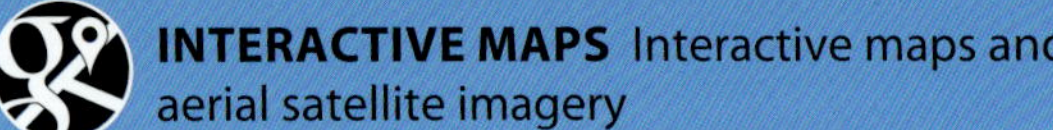
INTERACTIVE MAPS Interactive maps and aerial satellite imagery

QUIZZES Ten multiple choice questions that are automatically graded and emailed for teacher assessment

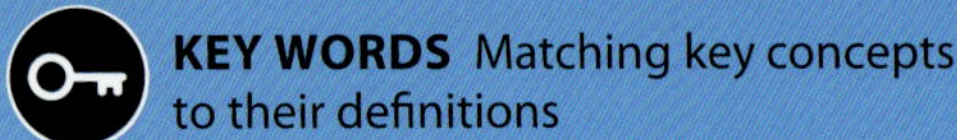
KEY WORDS Matching key concepts to their definitions

VIDEOS

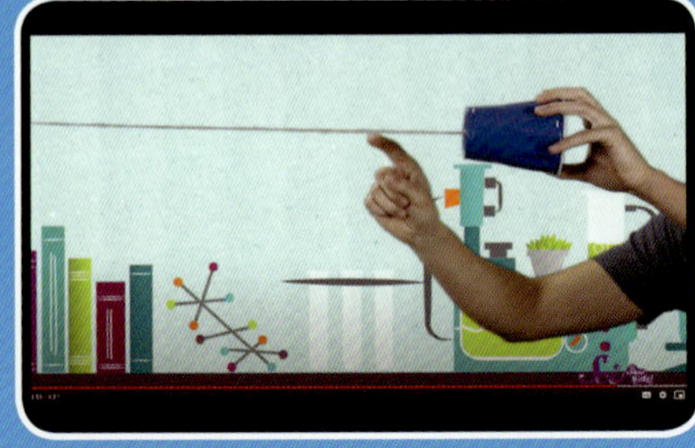

WEBLINKS

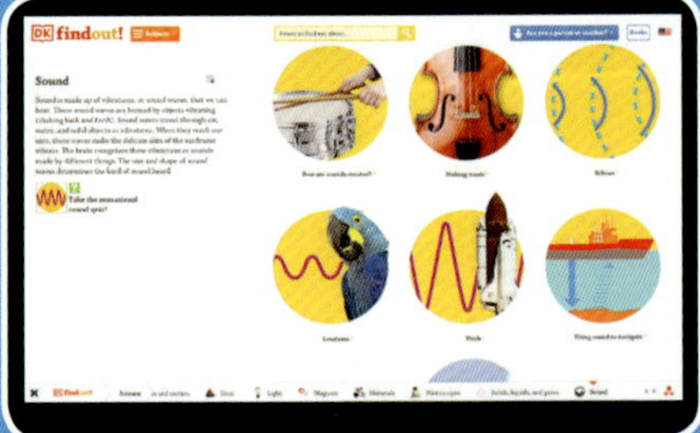

SLIDESHOWS

QUIZZES

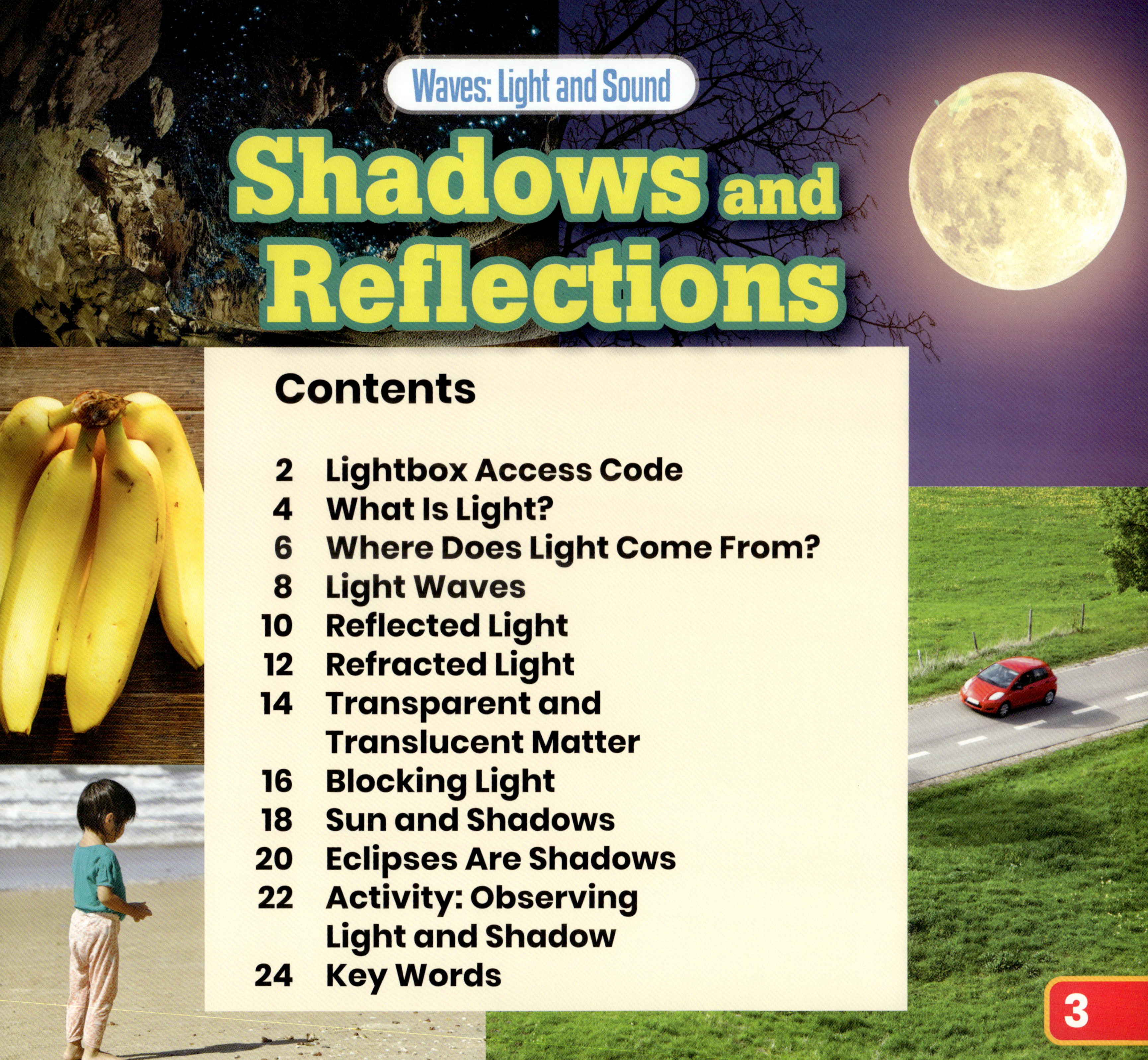

Waves: Light and Sound

Shadows and Reflections

Contents

What Is Light?

Light is brightness. It shows you the world. Without light, we could not see.

Because of light, you can see the flowers and butterflies outside. You can play with your toys inside.

Some animals **make** their own **light**.

Some jellyfish glow in the dark.

Fireflies glimmer at night.

Glowworms look like twinkling lights.

Most living things need light from the Sun.

Where Does Light Come From?

There are many sources of light on Earth. The main source is the Sun.

The Sun is a huge ball of hot gas in the sky. Its light shines down on the entire world. It gives light and heat to all living things.

People use **technology** to make light.

We turn a lamp on at home. A light bulb glows.

Flashlights help us see when it is dark.

Light Waves

All light sources make light waves. We see them as colors. All the colors together make white light.

Light waves move in straight lines until they hit matter. Everything around us is made of matter. You are made of matter, too.

Matter absorbs some light and reflects the rest. We see only the light waves that are reflected. This is how we see colors.

When we see **color**, we see **reflected light** waves.

Bananas look yellow. They absorb all other colors and reflect yellow light waves.

A red car appears red because it reflects red light waves.

Pumpkins reflect orange light waves and absorb the other colors.

Reflected Light

Not everything that shines is a light source. A mirror reflects light. It can also change its path. Moving a mirror changes light's direction.

The Moon does not make light. It only reflects sunlight. When you see the Moon in the sky, you are seeing reflected light from the Sun.

Moonlight takes about **1.3 seconds** to reach Earth.

Refracted Light

Not all matter absorbs or reflects light. Some matter allows light to pass through. For example, light travels through air and water.

When light travels through matter, it is sometimes refracted. To refract light is to bend it. Different types of matter make light waves bend in different ways.

A lens **refracts** light. We use **lenses** every day.

Our eyes have lenses. We would not be able to see without them.

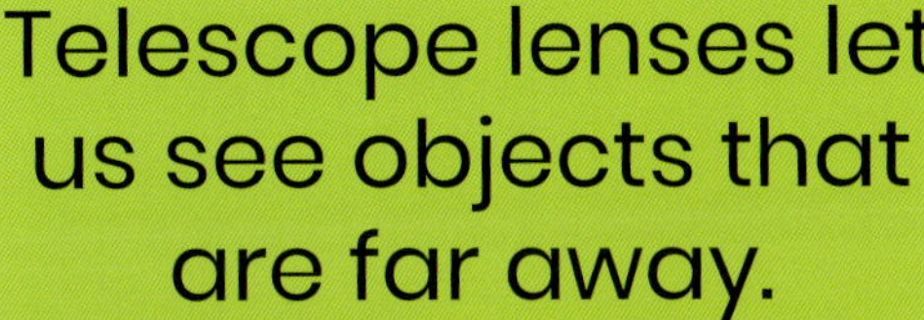

Telescope lenses let us see objects that are far away.

We use microscope lenses to see very small things.

Transparent and Translucent Matter

Transparent matter lets all light through. It does not block light. We see clearly through it. Air, water, and glass are transparent.

Translucent matter lets only some light through. A plastic milk jug is translucent. We can see if there is milk inside. We cannot see the milk clearly.

The Skydeck at Willis Tower in Chicago, Illinois, lets visitors stand on transparent glass floors.

Light passes better through **thin matter** than **thick matter**.

A thin layer of plastic wrap is transparent. You see everything through it.

You cannot see through an entire roll of plastic wrap. It is too thick. It is no longer transparent.

Blocking Light

Some matter blocks light completely. No light passes through. Matter that blocks light is called opaque.

Most objects are opaque. Walls and wooden doors are opaque. Tables and chairs are opaque.

Blocking light makes a dark area behind an object. The dark area is called a shadow.

You are **opaque**, too, and your **shadow** is unique.

Find a bright light. Use your hands to create shadow puppets on the wall. Can you make a rabbit?

A silhouette is the outline of a shadow. Draw silhouettes of your friends on paper. Can people tell who each silhouette belongs to?

Sun and Shadows

Most shadows are formed when matter blocks sunlight. When you face the Sun, your shadow is behind you. If the Sun is behind you, then your shadow is in front.

As the **Sun** moves through the sky, **shadows** change.

The Sun is overhead at noon. This means it is directly above you. Shadows at noon are short.

In the evening, the Sun is near the horizon. Its light reaches you at an angle. Evening shadows are long.

Eclipses Are Shadows

Earth travels around the Sun. The Moon travels around Earth. Both Earth and the Moon are opaque. Sometimes, they cast shadows on each other as they travel. These are called eclipses.

A lunar eclipse happens when Earth gets between the Sun and the Moon. Earth's shadow covers the Moon. A solar eclipse happens when the Moon moves between Earth and the Sun. It casts its small shadow on Earth. The Sun disappears completely during a total solar eclipse.

There is a **total solar eclipse** about every **18 months**.

Activity

Observe Light and Shadow

Objects are transparent, transluscent, or opaque. See how light passes through different objects.

Supplies

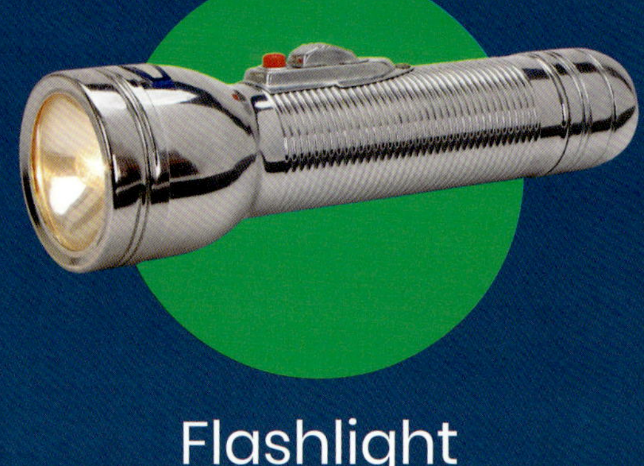

Flashlight

Clear glass cup

White paper

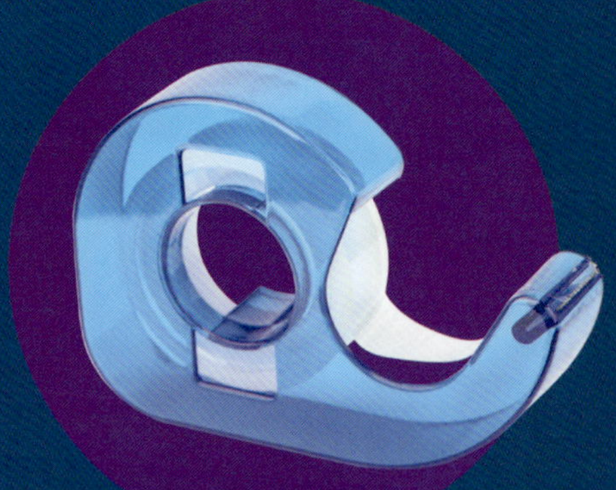

Tape

Notebook

Blown-up balloon

Construction paper

STEP 1 Tape the white paper to a wall.

STEP 2 Shine the flashlight on the paper. Look at the circle of light. Draw what you see in a notebook.

STEP 3 Place an object between the flashlight and the paper. How has the circle of light changed? Is it brighter or dimmer? Draw what you see.

STEP 4 Do this with other objects. Try to predict which objects will let light pass through them. To predict is to tell something before it takes place.

KEY WORDS

Research has shown that as much as 65 percent of all written material published in English is made up of 300 words. These 300 words cannot be taught using pictures or learned by sounding them out. They must be recognized by sight. This book contains 117 common sight words to help young readers improve their reading fluency and comprehension. This book also teaches young readers several important content words, such as proper nouns. These words are paired with pictures to aid in learning and improve understanding.

Page	Sight Words First Appearance
4	and, because, can, could, is, it, light, not, of, play, see, shows, the, we, what, with, without, world, you, your
5	animals, at, from, in, like, look, make, most, need, night, own, some, their, things
6	a, all, are, come, does, down, Earth, gives, its, many, on, there, to, where
7	help, home, people, turn, us, use, when
8	around, as, how, lines, made, move, only, that, them, they, this, together, too, until, white
9	car, other
10	about, also, change, seconds, takes
12	air, different, example, for, sometimes, through, water, ways
13	away, be, day, every, eyes, far, have, let, our, small, very, would
14	if
15	an, than
16	no
17	each, find, hands, paper, tell, who
18	face, then
19	above, long, means, near
20	between, both, gets, these

Page	Content Words First Appearance
4	brightness, butterflies, flowers, toys
5	dark, fireflies, glowworms, jellyfish, Sun
6	ball, gas, heat, sky, sources
7	flashlights, lamp, light bulb, technology
8	colors, light waves, matter
9	banana, pumpkins
10	mirror, Moon, moonlight, sunlight
13	lens, microscope, objects, telescope
14	Chicago, floors, glass, Illinois, jug, milk, Skydeck, visitors, Willis Tower
15	layer, plastic wrap, roll
16	area, chairs, doors, shadow, tables, walls
17	friends, outline, rabbit, shadow puppets, silhouette
19	angle, evening, horizon, noon
20	eclipses, lunar eclipse, solar eclipse
21	months

Published by Smartbook Media Inc.
14 Penn Plaza, 9th Floor New York, NY 10122
Website: www.openlightbox.com

Library of Congress Control Number: 2020937080

ISBN 978-1-5105-5405-4 (hardcover)
ISBN 978-1-5105-5406-1 (multi-user eBook)

Printed in Guangzhou, China
1 2 3 4 5 6 7 8 9 0 24 23 22 21 20

052020
110819

Project Coordinator: Priyanka Das
Designer: Jean Faye Marie Rodriguez

Every reasonable effort has been made to trace ownership and to obtain permission to reprint copyright material. The publisher would be pleased to have any errors or omissions brought to its attention so that they may be corrected in subsequent printings.

The publisher acknowledges Getty Images, iStock, and Shutterstock as the primary image suppliers for this title.

First published by Crabtree Publishing Company in 2014.